# Porthole
## David Borrott

smith|doorstop

Published 2015 by
smith|doorstop Books
The Poetry Business
Bank Street Arts
32-40 Bank Street
Sheffield S1 2DS

ISBN 978-1-910367-43-8
Typeset by Utter
Printed by MPG Biddles

**Acknowledgements**
Some of these poems have been published previously. Thanks to the
editors of the following magazines, anthologies and websites: *The North*,
*The Interpreter's House*, *Watermark* (Flax Books), *Solstice & Heavenly
Bodies* (Beautiful Dragons Press), *CAST: The Poetry Business Book of
New Contemporary Poets* (smith|doorstop), Magmapoetry.com and
kimmoorepoet.wordpress.com.

Thanks to Matt Bryden, Elizabeth Burns, Sarah Corbett & Kim Moore.

smith|doorstop Books are a member of Inpress:
www.inpressbooks.co.uk. Distributed by Central Books Ltd.,
99 Wallis Road, London E9 5LN

The Poetry Business gratefully acknowledges the support
of Arts Council England.

Supported by
ARTS COUNCIL
ENGLAND

# Contents

*to Rachel*

# Narada

*(after a parable by Swami Vivekananda)*

So Narada said to sky-like Krishna,
'Lord, show me Maya,' as they left
the fertile land and entered an arid place;
sand, each grain unique, blew about their feet
and raced before them towards the west
where jagged mountains tore the sky-line.
Krishna said 'I am thirsty, Narada, can you fetch me water?'
and Narada went but at the water fountain
he met Michelle from human resources
who was beautiful as the flight of birds
and she told him of a gig that evening
close by; so they went together
and for a pizza beforehand
which they both enjoyed tremendously
and Narada forgot his waiting master.
The next morning, he sold assurances
and bought futures and became a valuable asset
for the company. He and Michelle dated,
married, mortgaged a house and raised children.
So it was that 12 years later the dam
above their house burst and water gushed
through their upstairs bedroom. Narada
flailed in the flood, his children clinging
to his shoulders and Michelle beside him.
They swam towards safety when a surge swept him
under, he rose gagging and alone,
in tears he drifted to the crumbling bank
and there Krishna helped him to his feet.
'My child,' said his blue master, 'where is the water?
You have been gone for half an hour.'

## Pigeons

I love the shiftings of my neighbour's pigeons
as they swirl a ragged loop above the houses
as if in a vortex or on a long string,
grey against the grey sky, orbiting
the coop where their owner drags
on his morning smoke and follows as we all do
the flex and oscillation of their flight.

It's the unification of the group that amazes me –
how each individual bird invents the flock
pulling together to become a spun set of dancers
stretching the edge of the turn or lifting
to redefine the cumulative angle, the joined geometry that
flouts the television aerials, muscles past the pines
in the conjugation of their joyful ellipse,

each giving way to the general pattern
to become something more than themselves –
a single swooping transport, of one spirit
flying, as words can ally in a crowd of words,
if just momentarily before the leader turns leaden,
the noose closes and each bird comes to earth
on that derelict shit stained hut that everybody hates.

## Ultrasound

With four point five megahertz of clarity,
through jelly on your lifting bulge,
we see into our future: a prophecy
that flutters against your gut,
a resonance vaguely like ourselves.

For you, it is already here:
For me, it is as intangible as tomorrow,
as if far away, submersed amid oceanic depths,
a greening on the scope,
looming, rising on anticipation's winch.

Tonight I may place my hand
on the projection of your belly
and feel only a warmth,
as one feels casually on the bonnet of a car
that has been somewhere, has somewhere to go.

## Self Portrait with Fiddling Death

*(After Arnold Böcklin)*

Death stands behind me fiddling,
by fiddling I mean playing the violin.
Death is his usual skeletal self,
imaginatively thin but a palpable symbol
and stark: the drumlins of his old skull,
the darkness flowing through his ribs.

The music fills the room like a fog,
it hangs in droplets from the furniture,
dampens my palette, muddies the paint.
His violin is curved like a scorpion's sting.
his bow cradles the bridge, drifting over
the strange ocean it is pulling in.

Surely he misses some notes his fing-
er-bones jar on the chords or pluck
an off string, but I know the tune anyway
As the darkness behind us ferments
how similar we become, our open smiles,
after a while it's only the violin
that distinguishes us.

# Gelotophyllis

*'Let Bear, house of Bear rejoice with Gelotophyllis an herb which
drank in wine and myrrh causes excess of laughter'*
– Christopher Smart, *Jubilate Agno, Fragment D*


passed me a smoke, his mix, harsh jazz,
one brief taste and it has you by the hair,
cooks you like brisket bathing in hot oil,
– I could only sit and laugh,

actually more subtle, electric wraparounds
a yellowing of the eyesight,
so that the road was gold, the dank bench
we bobbed on, especially the trees,

being canopied and above ourselves;
we coughed at shoppers,
their boots clopped ringtones
as they shied from our burning fingers.

## Bag of Winds

I'm ready to blow you away
with my bag of winds.

I can quarter the sky,
hold it in this hessian sack:

one is like walking into a freezer,
one an oven, one a spring meadow,

one the stretched back of the sea.
I can loosen a breeze

to unsettle your hats, set your hair flying
or a gale that will chase you indoors.

I can turn your skin to gooseflesh
or lull you with an air that caresses

so peacefully it's almost not there.
Here's a rainy squall that wants attention,

here's an icy blast, it's not all talk,
don't call me windbag, it's in my fingertips

if I can just undo the knots.

## 'felicitous blending of figure and landscape'

Two youths are fighting on the high street.
One with a logo of blood on his white shirt,
the other's fists are tight as apples;
a clench of excitement runs through the watching people,
their faces like a row of broken plates.
Dummies in the glass extend the crowd –
'Next' says the shop sign.

On the stone plinth of the war memorial,
a woman with XXXL breasts is smoking.
She rests earthmotherly on the steps.
Smoke rises around her like billowing hair,
or her own ghost filtering into being,
its intricacies merge with a sycamore
as she stands out against the monument.

A man is pissing down an alley.
It is night and a soft untroublesome rain persists.
Street lights reflect in the puddles,
touches of orange amongst the grey and brown.
His fawn jacket is darker at the shoulders,
his half-cocked trousers are shadowy, vague.
It is almost as if he hovered there on the jet of his stream.

## Wolf Fell

You stand on the edge with your wife,
your balding head a wholesome colour
in the November sunshine. You are
taking a picture of Wolf Fell,
air-fuddled in the distance.

Here is the order in which these things shall be lost:
your remaining hair, the photograph, you, your wife,
this prominence, Wolf Fell, the air, the sunshine.

## Rare

My steak will go back to the cow
as a jigsaw piece into a puzzle,
it will fit perfectly, uncooking,
all the steam sliding down into the flesh.

The cow will go back to its field
which becomes a prairie, slowly like horns
growing the world expands and the herd
thunders across it, hooves beating, beating

until the wildness is pounded back in
and I am hiding in darkness, smearing
in ochre the shape of a beast
that is terror and blood and the tip of my courage.

## Southern Cross

Darkness and us moved high above the Pacific,
our 747 a corridor of stale air
swollen with the helium of sleep.
I dreamt a thousand miles and woke
to the window's stare, its coldness
crossing the glass to my hand, my eye.

The ocean below us dark as a fairy story,
a paradise of islands, forgotten boats,
of journeys under our journey, our hulking plane
a red flashing dot above their tilting masts,
and above me suddenly the stars, Crux unmistakable
a neon welcome to the South.

Then a meteor charged the earth
slashing that constellation, Just for myself alone,
mouth widening to accept a wonder,
as if the sky had said yes, my reflected face
echoing the shock as that shining tick
ignites a hemisphere.

And knowing it was random – falling dust,
knowing outside it meant nothing; that meant nothing
to my keening head bursting with the fire of it.

## Aquarium with Toddler

Lit-up rectangles filled with the weird:
a baggy-headed octopus with a salad of legs;
lobsters, big-clawed, like futuristic war machines;
pinstripe and leopard print shoals.

In the giant tank the flat-bellied sharks
fly over us, swallowing the bloodless water.
Glum piranhas congregate by the bubble filter,
A ray hangs like a shirt on the line.

What happened to the infinite expanse?
Where is the push of the tide? Jellyfish
bulge and flutter like see-through hearts,
crabs fold up against the perspex.

Safe in his pushchair, Thomas sees the blue TVs
hears the bathroom sounds, a mish-mash
wattage of fish floating past him, dancing
for his fingers, shrunk by his tapping.

## People in Manchester

The blue busdriver
points his fishtank
towards Wythenshawe

Two plain lovers lick
one vanilla cornet

In a hurry,
her ponytail's a metronome

Office junior
pondering
a baked potato

In various grey suits,
businessmen and pigeons

Outside the Arndale,
pink trails
lead back to a spillage

On the mobile,
maybe his voice
is in Macao

In Piccadilly Gardens,
a boy spins like a bobbin;
the city warps about him

On Mkt St,
an overdose of faces

Two women with a pram;
one has nowhere to put her hands

Man U, Man U,
his beer flush is devotional

Lovely overflowing to blubbery,
her belt, in stars, says 'oddess'

The tram's metallic charge
bears 15 people away

Acts of random laziness,
the chewing gum art installation
goes on for miles

Abandoning the Science Museum,
a spot of rain
becomes her bindi

Streets are slickened,
windows bubblewrapped,
his orange anorak is almost acceptable

On the current of people,
such dark and gaudy shields
float over them

Rain decorates a queue of skips
on Granby Road,
the pepper in my pasty

Leading the troop of commuters,
he carries the Evening News
as if it were a baton

Around lit doorways,
the smokers' conversations
are febrile scarves

The chain on the security camera
clangs repeatedly;
it is one million o'clock

# Flood

*(after a line by Lorca)*

*Each night the sea covers the earth*
it rises above the sleeping houses.
Listen, its waves are lifting the rooftiles.
Tonight, I am pulled between the wrecks of buildings,
around the fronds of trees,
the coral of the liquefied gardens,
drowning slowly in the breathless night.
The sky is a vast ship passing above me,
barnacles stud its hull, one porthole shines.

## Boggart

The rock, in fact, was somewhere down a lane,
I went the wrong way but still got there.
I remember brambles, a spider on a gate
a mud path looping a field, then I found it
And under it the ghoul, held by its weight,
nobody at the farm, nobody in the fields.
Are we not all held down by a rock?
I thought and touched the stone, which had no
markings except what time had laid on it.

Of course, this is a thing of the mind,
one has to tune the thinking to unveil,
the lank fiend in his burrow, his furred limbs
the crowing mouth sipping the crack of light
as I prise the boulder up – he sizzles free
and I take in that hatred of imprisonment.
Imagine the surge, I can't control it yet but when I do
havoc will stampede through my skull
and such mad words will rocket from my beak.

## *Explorers*

The astronaut jogs a marathon without leaving her treadmill, her hair floats above her like a movie star's, stars are turning outside the cupola, really she has run three times around the world.

On a Pacific island Amelia injured eats shellfish, the ejecta of the tide, her leg won't work, it is like a broken wing, then the tide and the shellfish eat her.

Emily dashes towards the church, it is raining and her shawl is useless, inside there is so much captured emptiness, she has to stand in the porch letting the rain finish colouring her boots.

# Endurance

I drive uphill through moth-rich lanes,
Polaris in my sights, a bubble of colour
about me – hedgerow green flares up and dies.
Through a town with its eyes sealed shut,
the cars derelict, the houses bare rock.
Only the crossing beacons toss and catch their light.
Then the heights open, Lancashire splayed-out,
splashes of neon where it merges with the sea.

A luminous belt hugs the hills to the north
as dawn rolls round under the edge,
half a prism, smudged orange, lime, loose blue,
a clump of Queen Anne's Lace tattoos the sky.
It's chill and quiet, my engine contracts,
there's no one here to confirm this reality,
only me holding onto it, with Pegasus overhead,
the whole sky a twist away from blanching.

The small hours are malleable, closer to elsewhere,
so cold I have a vision of Shackleton on his floe,
far out, the crumpled ship locked in ice, these hills
could be bergs breaching the pack, the coastal lights
a frozen seam glistening. I slide back down
into soft flights of snow; there's one truck –
a whale shouldering through the thin ice of the leads;
these bushes, blocks skewed from the pressure ridge.

## Summit

I am playing Beethoven to the spiders
that skulk in the high grass at the hilltop,
they are busy with their smooth lines
or purr in a nitch, owning new trapezoid
fantasticals, honeycombed outlayings.

Clouds are giving in to the blueness, a heat haze
obscuring the valley like squalls of rain
What do you think spiders? Could you build
such a web as this music, pulling the silver thread
out of yourself, splicing the nettle leaves.

I could tramp along the ridge side
hoping some gust of air might reach me
but I want to hear what Beethoven does
to make the piano lift up, the keys flexing
like heads of corn, the notes taking off like seeds.

## Barnard's Star

If you look keenly enough you can see
the future falling towards you, as E.E.
Barnard did in nineteenth century Tennessee.

Eyeing his way upwards out of poverty,
he cast his telescope across the nights'
uncertain rivers and hooked like fish

the comets edging in from the invisible,
earning prizes to build a house and a reputation.
He found a loop, a galaxy, Jupiter's fifth moon –

the first since Galileo, and catalogued the sky's
'dark markings': nebulae of gas, including B33
the Horsehead in Orion, and closer Barnard's star

which slithers across Ophiuchus, the serpent bearer,
through the fluff of the Local Bubble
towards us at eighty-eight miles per second.

Think of all that momentum, an embering sun,
six light years off. Perhaps, in the ethereal future,
if we've not gone back to caves or egressed reality,

we'll mine it for energy. Because we claim
what comes our way, naming, owning, using –
as the snake charmer, Ophiuchus, milks his asp

or sets it, emergent, to dance for rupees,
until with eyes lit up we sway before it.

# Umbrellas

*(After the painting by Dorothy Brett in Manchester Art Gallery)*

It wasn't raining but umbrella
the Bloomsbury Set sat umbrella
on the blank lawn under umbrella
umbrellas, as if each unfurled sunshade
were an intellectual halo, an aura umbrella
in pink or night blue or pale leaf yellow;
such sharp spoked wings, almost demonic
umbrella despite the pastels. Centred on Lady Ottoline,
the conversation is languorous umbrella.
One lounging shadow has closed his orange parasol
to demonstrate how idiosyncrasy umbrella
is misdiagnosed as genius.
One umbrella is a palm tree
because nature is important. A man holds a white book
in his long white hand, his hat and beard
preclude the need for any sunshade umbrella
but his is the biggest, proudly
umbrella he clutches its stem.

## Emptying the Dishwasher

Taking a bowl into the palm of my hand
manoeuvring its hollow shape to the cupboard
not a chore – an exhilaration:
The arc of the movement, a bird's flight
into the nest of bowls; the back bent
in yogic posture as the dawn ambers,
the kitchen heating with my focus.

These fingers directing the cutlery
are metalsmiths. This grasp and thrust
of the forearm, placing exactly each cup,
is not mechanical but so pure it is as if
there were no arm, only the will directing
the flying crockery to lift and land.
Errorless as breath, a concentrated moment
that will not drop like the rest, that will not
break into fragments on the old stone floor.

## Pigafetta and the Patagonians

After two months we saw a giant ten spans high
dancing, singing, throwing sand over his head
with yellow tattooed eye-patches, a red
ring skirting his face, white painted hair –
we gave him a mirror, he was terrified;
as we all are to see our true self clearly.

Here are seven facts about these folk
called Tehuelche or Aonikenk or Pathagoni.
1. Nomadic they followed the guanaco herds across the pampas, living only in
tents made of guanaco hide.
2. Archers, their bows were strung with gut, their arrows tipped with flint,
tipped with poison.
3. When sick they dipped an arrow two feet down their gullet and vomited a
green spew.
4. A very agile race who do no harm. They were giants, so tall our tallest barely
made their waist. See also: de Weert, van Noort, Knivet, Falkner and Byron.
5. The women carry the possessions, loaded like asses, their breasts hang down
half a cubit.
6. At death, ten devils appear to dance around them and a greater devil, most
vigorous in his excitement, called Setebos. They paint themselves like these
devils.
7. They are now vanished into history, their successors overrun by cattle
ranchers spreading southwards from Fray Bentos.

They suited themselves with llama skins,
stuffed their boots with straw against the cold.
The Captain-General called them Bigfoot
and from this the whole region, Patagonia.
We tricked two, offering them irons
such as malefactors wear, these
they could not carry, their arms
being full of knick-knacks, so we clamped

them to their shins and caught them thus.
After that arrows were all their conversation.
One came as trophy on our vessel,
reciting the Hail Mary and kissing the cross –
he was the first to die in the Pacific.

And the eyes are other and the head is her
and the teeth are phor and the arm is mar
and the hand is cheni and the breast is ochii
and the penis is scachet and sex is johoi
and the buttocks are hoii and the heart is thol
(All these words are pronounced in the throat)
and gold is pelpeli and the sea is aro
and fire is ghialeme and water holi
and the stars are settere and the wind oni.

# Notes

'Narada' – Swami Vivekananda's (1863-1902) thoughts influenced Gandhi and much of modern Hinduism. According to Vedantic Hinduism the common world that we accept as reality is an illusion, this illusion is called Maya.

'Endurance' – Ernest Shackleton (1874-1922) was one of the foremost Antarctic explorers, his ship 'Endurance' was trapped and crushed by ice.

'Pigafetta and the Patagonians' – Antonio Pigafetta was a participant in, and chronicler of, Magellan's voyage which made the First Circumnavigation of the World (1519-22). Pigafetta recorded some of the words of the peoples he encountered.